CAPPADOCIA
The Cradle of Civilization

ÖMER DEMİR
Staff Member of the International Society for the
Investigation of Ancient Civilizations

1995

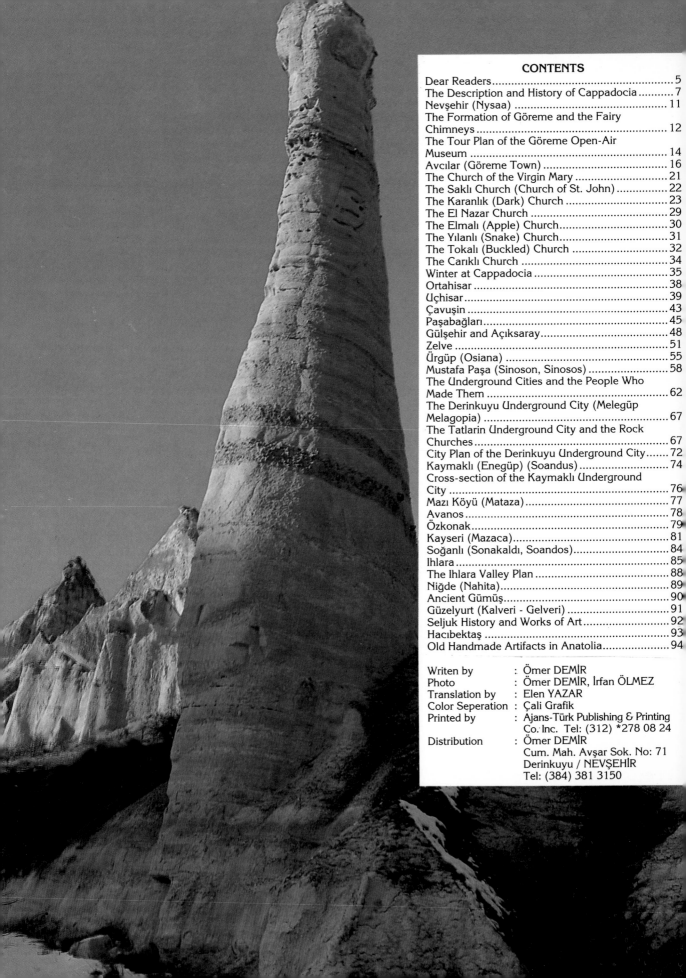

CONTENTS

Writen by   : Ömer DEMİR
Photo   : Ömer DEMİR, İrfan ÖLMEZ
Translation by   : Elen YAZAR
Color Seperation : Çali Grafik
Printed by   : Ajans-Türk Publishing & Printing
                   Co. Inc. Tel: (312) *278 08 24
Distribution   : Ömer DEMİR
                   Cum. Mah. Avşar Sok. No: 71
                   Derinkuyu / NEVŞEHİR
                   Tel: (384) 381 3150

DEAR READERS

*To date, various works have been published by different authors concerning the Cappadocia Region, but most of these have not satisfied the Turkish and foreign visitors to the Cappadocia Region. The information given is insufficient. This situation disturbed me very much. There is a need for a book that will present the Cappadocia Region in all its aspects and with the most minute details. I met Dr. Martin Urban, the German geologist and tourism writer who came to Turkey between 1968 to 1973. He was making studies in the Cappadocia Region to gather information to put in his book called **Underground City** and I assisted him. His successful activities in the Cappadocia Region and his support of me accelerated my activities and today I have a lot of new information. Thus, this book arose from the need to present an historical and tourism paradise in the light of new information.*

I owe a debt of gratitude to those who expended efforts in the preparation of my book, first of all to the people of Cappadocia who were unstinting in their assistance to me, to Dr. Martin Urban and furthermore, to Mr. Oktay Gürel, Managing Director of the Ajans-Türk Printing House and to all the personnel, due to their interest and assistance in the printing of this work. I am presenting this work, that is the product of my lengthy studies between 1968 to 1992, to you, my esteemed readers.

If I have been helpful, then I will consider myself to be fortunate.

Ömer DEMİR

DERİNKUYU

THE DESCRIPTION AND HISTORY OF CAPPADOCIA

Millions of years ago, with the eruption within Cappadocia of the Erciyes Mountain to the east and the Hasan Mountains to the west, the history of Cappadocia commenced in the periods when humanity first set foot in the region after the lava spread over the region cooled off. Çatalhöyük, connected to Konya in the northern mountain plateaus of the Taurus Mountains, was discovered by J. Melleart in 1958. A nine to ten thousand year old Neolithic Age settlement was found there with the excavation undertaken in 1965. Today the remains found in this excavation of the "Plump Woman" goddess statuettes, the refined women's jewelry, the colored ceramic objects, and the pots and pans give exceptional ideas concerning the culture and past of the oldest people in the area. The Topaklı Höyük (tumulus) excavations were undertaken between 1968 to 1977. Here were obtained pieces of baked clay and bones from 3500 B.C. and some pieces from A.D. 394. Furthermore, in the excavations undertaken by the Nevşehir Museum Directorate in 1991 at the Zank Höyük, twenty kilometers to the north of Avanos, Associate Professor Hüseyin Sever, the Museum Director Şeracettin Şahin, Archaeologists Halis Yenipınar and Murat Ertuğrul Gülyaz found kitchen containers, pots and the spindle whorls and weights used on the weaving looms belonging to the early Bronze Age. Great importance was placed on the making of pots and pans in these periods. The makers of pots and pans continue the same art even today in Avanos County by using the former methods of rotating wheels made of wood.

A powerful Hittite State was established by the joining together of the Proto-Hittites and the people of Neşa, who were living spread out in this region, and the uniting of their cultures. This powerful state continued until 1200 B.C. Hattusa was their capital city. We obtain the most extensive information concerning the Hittite civilizations from the written sources that were extracted from excavations at Hattusa and at Kanesh in Kayseri.

The invasions of Anatolia started in 1200 B.C. and the Hittite State was burned, destroyed and eliminated. The remains of the conflagration in those days can still be seen at Boğazköy, Alacahöyük and Alişar. After the destruction of the Great Hittite State, the beylic state was established in Anatolia and for a long period of time it remained un-

claimed. The Phrygians, who were famous for raising horses in Central Anatolia, took over the administration in the eighth century B.C. We do not have extensive information concerning from where the Phrygians came, where they settled when they first migrated to Anatolia and later on how they were able to found a powerful state. However, we know that the Phrygians entered Anatolia from Europe by means of the straits and according to the historian Herodotus, when the Phrygians were in Europe they were called Brygs or Birgs.

After the Phrygians, Cappadocia was occupied for a period of time by the Medes, but around the middle of the sixth century B.C., the Mede Empire suddenly collapsed and in 547 B.C. all of Anatolia came under the rule of the Persians. It was administered with the state method by governors who were called *Satraps* by the ancient Greeks and who were given the name of *Khshatrapa* in the Persian countries. There were *satrapies* whose number did not fall below twenty at the time of

the Persians. The satrapies were attached to a large kingdom. They would give their taxes annually in the form of horses, gold and silver talents. *Katpatukya* was the name given to Cappadocia by the Persians. Katpatukya had the meaning of "Beautiful Horse Country" in the Persian language. Cappadocia, that was within the Daskleion Satrapy, would pay an annual tax of 360 silver Talents to the large kingdom.

Alexander the Great occupied the southern portion of Cappadocia in 333 B.C., appointed a Persian by the name of Sabiktas as the Satrap and continued directly to the south for his great campaign. Approximately one year later, Ariarethes I became the king of Cappadocia, by obtaining the support of the people. Even though Ariarethes I expanded Cappadocia's boundaries to the Black Sea in the north and up to the Euphrates River in the east, Perdiccas, one of Alexander's step-sons, marched to Cappadocia and once again took over the rule. The great empire that Alexander the Great had founded started to weaken with his death, because there was not an heir to take his place. It was required for the commanders, who were called the Diadochi in history, to administer

with unity and cooperation the large empire that had been established. However, after the struggles of the small kingdoms founded by the Diadochi, which lasted for approximately 300 years, they were ended in 30 B.C. by the Romans who abolished the kingdoms of the final Hellenistic period.

Ariarethes II, the adopted son of Ariarethes I left the country after the death of Ariarethes I and the campaign of Perdiccas. In 301 B.C. he returned and saved Southern Cappadocia which Alexander the Great had occupied and ensured unity and cooperation. The boundaries of the country were expanded, especially during the periods of Ariarethes III, IV and V. The Cappadocian King Ariarethes V brought Greek artists and intellectuals to the palace and the Hellenistic culture became dominant in Cappadocia, in particular, the cities of Mazaca (Kayseri) and Tyana (Kemerhisar) became the sites of Hellenism. Cappadocia encountered a loss of power and it gradually started to enter under the influence of Rome with the death of Ariarethes V. Cappadocia frequently changed hands after this between the Roman and the Pontus Kingdoms. Cappadocia met with considerable

damage in these wars. In 47 B.C. Caesar's army, that opened war on the Pontus Kingdom, settled in Mazaca and stayed here for a period of time. They took over Southern Pontus. Mazaca's (Kayseri) name was changed and it started to be called Caesarea Mazaca at the time of Caesar and it completely became a Roman state in 17 B.C.

Jesus was thirty years old when he announced Christianity in Palestine. Jesus was crucified when Pontius Pilate, Rome's Governor of Jerusalem, accused that Jesus would found a new state in Palestine. However, Jesus's disciples left Palestine and spread to various regions and tried to spread Christianity by interpreting it. St. Gregory Nazianzen (Nenezilli), St. Gregory of Nyssa (Nevşehir) and St. Basil the Great, who were the important religious men born in the Cappadocia Region at the time, developed Christianity rapidly in Central Anatolia and placed importance on the construction of churches and monasteries. The first places of worship in general were in the form of a small monastery, more accurately they were places of retreat. They did not have a significant architectural structure. In general these places of worship

were constructed in the valleys, in the stream beds or in places that were difficult to find, because Christianity had still not been liberated. There were rebellions and civic turmoil in Rome in the years around A.D. 310 and Constantine suppressed these revolts and became the emperor of Rome. Christianity was liberated in A.D. 313 when Constantine became the emperor and later Rome's capital city was moved to Byzantium (İstanbul). The religion developed rapidly in Cappadocia after the acceptance of Christianity and it entered the religious influence of the İstanbul Patriarchate and continued the construction of churches and monasteries.

The Byzantine Empire was the setting for important events domestically and abroad in the seventh century. In Arabia the Islamic religion was born, expanded and started to put pressure on the Byzantine borders. Within the country, the tendencies of the monks to worship icons to a idolatrous degree was paving the way to reactions. The Iconoclastic period started in A.D. 726 with a law promulgated by Leon III, and it continued for over 100 years, thus reducing the power of the churches and monasteries. Religious drawings were forbidden and churches and monasteries were closed down in this period. This situation continued until A.D. 843 when Empress Theodora once again made the use of icons unrestricted. New churches were constructed at the Göreme, Ihlara and Soğanlı Valleys with the freedom of icons. The interiors of these churches were decorated with frescoes that mentioned subjects in the Bible. The most beautiful churches and frescoes of the Byzantine period started to be made after this period. The construction of churches at Cappadocia continued up until the thirteenth century.

The religious beliefs of the Byzantines were not influenced and their worship was left unrestricted with the rapid conquering of Anatolia by the Seljuks in 1071. The churches and mosques that were constructed in the same locations and at the same time in this region are a symbol of how tolerantly the two societies regarded each other. It is possible to see an example of this at the Zelve ruins. There were so many churches, chapels and monasteries constructed at Cappadocia, that while it is not possible to give the exact number of these, it is estimated that over 400 were constructed. Most of the paintings at the churches were made after the Iconoclastic period. The paintings were either made based on a specific line of beauty in a classic manner or else only in a simple style that was showing the subject. Some of the churches as well were made in the framework of a certain plan and just as importance was placed on the construction of the interior, great pains were also taken for the external construction, such as the Domed Church at Soğanlı. At the time of the first Christians, other than the churches, monasteries and chapels were built at Cappadocia, importance was also placed on the construction of caves and by making small chapels in the interiors of these caves, they continued their religious worship here.

The armies of Caliph Ömer entered into the interior of Anatolia and fought successful battles between 717 to 718. Mesleme, one of Ömer's commanders, went as far as Kayseri and wrought severe losses on the Byzantine army. While these caves were used as a shelter against both this Islamic invasion and the Seljuks who entered Anatolia in 1071, after the Seljuks Turkicized Anatolia and recognized religious freedom for the Christians, these underground caves and secret places of worship lost their importance. The beylic period in Anatolia commenced after the breaking up of the Seljuks. The cities of Cappadocia changed hands among these beylics from time to time. After the Ottomans increased in size and became more powerful, they became a strong state that possessed all of Anatolia. The religious beliefs of the Christians were not influenced during the Ottoman period as well, but in this period the Christians did not display an effective religious development. In 1924, after the proclamation of the Republic and the population exchanges (between Turkey and Greece which followed the signing of the Treaty of Lausanne in 1923), the Christian group at Cappadocia came to an end to a great extent.

Very significant wonders have occurred at Cappadocia with the joining forces of history, nature and mankind. It is possible to gather in three separate categories the places visited that are of interest and liked by the tourists coming to the region.

1. The natural beauties, the fairy chimneys (a cone-shaped pillar of tuff capped with basalt) and the valleys which are unique in the world.

2. The rock churches with frescoes with portrayals that symbolize Jesus, the Virgin Mary, the saints and subjects from the Bible.

3. The underground cities, which are described as the eighth wonder of the world, whose construction it is estimated were started in the years before Christ and which were later made more extensive and were used both as secret places of worship and as shelters.

NEVŞEHİR (NYSSA)

Nevşehir (Nyssa) was founded in Central Anatolia in the Kızılırmak (Halys) valley on the slopes of Kahveci Mountain and its history dates back long before Christ. Its former name was Nyssa and later it became Muşkara.

The Hittites, who lived between 2000 to 1200 B.C., first of all settled in the interior part that constitutes the north of the Kızılırmak River and later they expanded the boundaries directly outside of the branches of the Kızılırmak River. In the seventh century B.C., after the collapse of the Hittites, Nevşehir was under the protection of the Assyrians some of the time and the Phrygians for part of the time. In 546 B.C. the Persian Emperor Cyrus added Nevşehir to his territories. In the sixth century B.C. all of Anatolia was added to the Persian Empire. In 333 B.C. the Macedonian Emperor, Alexander the Great destroyed the Persian Empire and took possession of these lands. Later, with the uniting of the boundaries of Kayseri, Niğde and Nevşehir, the Cappadocian Kingdom came into existence and ruled here. The capital city of this kingdom was called by the name of Mazaca which is the Kayseri Province of today. Roman sovereignty was accepted in the first century B.C. and Nevşehir was attached to the Roman Empire. After the Romans, there was also Byzantine rule at Nevşehir. As a matter of fact, the greatest number of works of art have remained from the Byzantine period in the lands of Nevşehir, with its rock churches, underground shelters and places of worship. At the time when Christianity first started to spread, those who were Christian experienced great oppression from the idolaters and they made a large number of shelters underground such as those at Derinkuyu, Kaymaklı, Doğala, Özkonak and Mazı to protect themselves and to secretly spread their religion.

In A.D. 313 after Constantine officially freed this religion, the underground caves were only used as a shelter against the invasions of tribes such as the Arabs and the Sassanids. Shelters lost their importance in the periods after this and the Christians abandoned and left these places and made hundreds of churches in the stone hollows in the Göreme, Soğanlı and Ihlara Valleys and settled in these places. Some of the events in the Bible were transferred as paintings in the interiors of these churches.

After the war between Alparslan and Romanus IV (Romanus Diogenes) in A.D. 1071, at the Battle of Malazgirt (Manzikert), Nevşehir was taken over by the Seljuks. Later, one of the Seljuk Sultans, Kılıçarslan II divided the land among his eleven sons and Nevşehir was given to his son Mesut. However, his brother Ruknettin took Nevşehir back from his brother in 1204. In 1308, after the Seljuks were completely destroyed, Nevşehir was possessed by the İlhanlıs. Afterwards, the rule of the Karamanoğlus and the Dulkadiroğlus was experienced in Nevşehir. It was conquered by the Ottomans with Yavuz Sultan Selim's putting an end to the Dulkadiroğlu's Beylic. Around the beginning of the seventeenth century, when Damat İbrahim Pasha, who was born in Nevşehir, entered the Ottoman Palace both as bridegroom and as Grand Vizier, this city whose former name was Muşkara, was given the name of Nevşehir, which has the meaning of New City. A number of development and construction activities were undertaken and khans, Turkish baths, madrasahs (theological schools attached to the mosques) and the Kurşunlu Mosque, that has a very interesting method of construction, are the main works of art that are remaining from the time of Damat İbrahim Pasha of Nevşehir.

Nevşehir was a county of Niğde Province up until 1954, when it became a province. In Nevşehir the main sources of income are carpet weaving and viticulture and in its surroundings are located the remains of the underground cities, the fairy chimneys, the rock churches, the monasteries and the caravanserais which are unique in the world.

THE FORMATION OF GÖREME AND THE FAIRY CHIMNEYS

Thousands of years ago when Erciyes Mountain was active, the lava that was cast forth covered an area of approximately 20,000 km². Afterwards, when it became an inactive volcano, this region encountered a tremendous wind and water erosion for hundreds of years.

As a result of this erosion, the soil was abraded and dragged away and the rocks which were able to withstand this abrasion were left uncovered. The small rock pieces that are hard and graveled remained on top of the larger rocks and formed the fairy chimneys of today.

The Christians who took shelter in the Göreme valley because of the Arab pressures gave it the name of *Göremi* which means "you cannot see here". Later on, this name was *Korama* and gradually it has come up until today in the form of *Göreme*.

Located between Nevşehir and Ürgüp in the Avcılar Valley that is at a distance of seventeen ki-lometers from Nevşehir and six kilometers from Ürgüp, the very different, interesting fairy chimneys and the rock churches are drawing the attention of those who come to the region. St. Paul considered Göreme to be more suitable for the training of missionaries. Formerly Göreme was perhaps more extensive, but today it is consisting of only one valley.

Göreme was one of the large centers of Christianity from the sixth century C.E. until around the end of the ninth century C.E. and there were around 400 churches. These are distributed in locations such as Zelve, Mustafa Paşa, Avcılar, Uçhisar, Ortahisar and Çavuşin. In fact, these villages that we have mentioned are very close to each other. The churches at Göreme are as follows: the Tokalı (Buckled) Church, the Çarıklı Church, the Karanlık (Dark) Church, the Church of the Virgin Mary, the Elmalı (Apple) Church, the Yılanlı (Snake) Church, the Church of St. Barbara and the El Nazar Church.

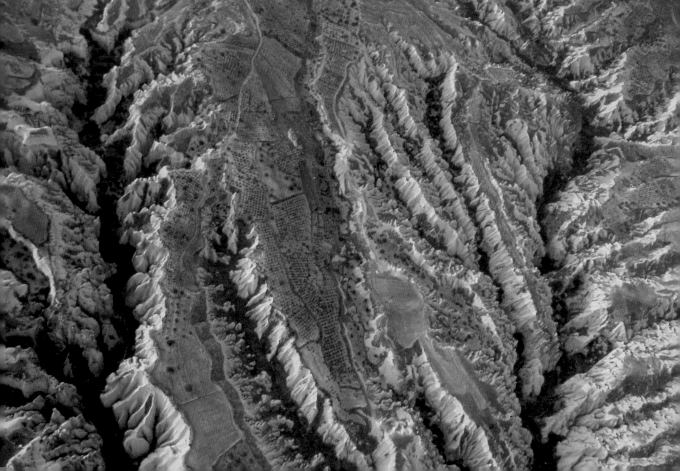

CHURCH OF THE VIRGIN MARY

PARKING AREA

TOKALI (BUCKLED) CHURCH

ÜRGÜP

NORTH

TICKET WINDOW

NUNNERY

NEVŞEHIR

ÇARIKLI CHURCH

KARANLIK (DARK) CHURCH

DINING HALL

ELMALI (APPLE) CHURCH

CHURCH OF ST. BARBARA

YILANLI (SNAKE) CHURCH

The Tour Plan ot the Göreme Open - Air Museum

AVCILAR (Göreme Town)

The town of Avcılar is 500 meters to the west of the Göreme rock churches and is a town that is living in the immediate proximity of the natural beauties and the historical remains within the Göreme Valley. This location, that is on an area of about 5 km², has fairy chimneys, one more beautiful than the other, rock hollows and churches remaining from the Iconoclastic period. Most of these churches were previously destroyed and only one or two of the churches with frescoes have been able to remain intact up until today.

The residents here are continuing their lives in close contact with these splendid fairy chimneys and rock hollows. Due to the fact that the winter season is cold and the summer is hot in this region, rooms made from cut stones have been added within some of the rock cavities which are protecting from the cold of winter and the heat of summer. Today some of these are also providing services to tourism as pensions.

To look at the fairy chimneys and the boundless beauties in the Cappadocia Region, it is necessary to look from the vineyards two kilometers to the west of the town or from the Uçhisar Citadel. The residents of Avcılar (Göreme) town have comprehended very well the importance of tourism and have assumed the job of providing services to tourism. Because of this, they have constructed hotels, motels, campsites and pensions with their own resources and they are assisting the domestic and foreign tourists who are coming to the region and are presenting to them the finest examples of Turkish hospitality.

Of the rock churches found here, the Kadir Durmuş Church is in a westerly direction from the town at Keşişdere. It was built on six columns and is a lovely church from the point of view of construction. There are no paintings in the interior.

The Yusuf Koç Church is in the same location and was hollowed out of a high fairy chimney and was used up until recently as a pigeon house. It is one of the churches built after the Iconoclastic period and has a transverse cross plan and two apses. The supports of the church have been destroyed, but the frescoes in the interior have remained in good condition. The internal construction and the paintings greatly resemble the Elmalı Church at the Open-Air Museum. The two churches which we have mentioned have been given the names of the landowners because they are within private property. Their original names are unknown. Furthermore, the town of Göreme was the scene of many civilizations in the period before Christ. The monumental Roman cemetery located in the center of the town has become the symbol of the town of Göreme.

THE CHURCH OF THE VIRGIN MARY

Before reaching the Göreme Open-Air Museum, one turns left next to the Tokalı Church. After going 100 meters more directly to the north, one reaches the Kılıçlar Valley that has a depth of thirty meters.

The Church of the Virgin Mary was constructed on the upper edge of this valley that has a lovely view.

Here is one of the churches that has experienced a tremendous amount of destruction from erosion.

The interior is entered by bending over because the entrance door to the church is low. There is a round stone door at the entrance door opening.

A tunnel was made next to this stone door and it is thought that this tunnel was a connection to the other churches.

At the Church of the Virgin Mary there are frescoes with many scenes from the Bible and reproduced in these frescoes are the Virgin Mary praying, Jesus praying, his crucifixion and the figures of the saints.

In many scenes in the frescoes, as pictures of the Virgin Mary were worked repeatedly, it has been called the Church of the Virgin Mary.

The Church of the Virgin Mary is one of the churches worth seeing at Göreme.

THE SAKLI CHURCH (CHURCH OF ST. JOHN)

The Saklı Church (Church of St. John) is located outside the town of Avcılar on the ridges on the right hand side, 300 meters before the Göreme Open-Air Museum. It is reached after climbing some 250 to 300 meters on the path going directly up the ridge. The carved church entrance door in the western portion of the hill is looking at the Zemi Valley. This church was hollowed out in such a slope of the hill that it is not possible to notice the church before arriving next to it.

The door of this church was closed by erosion and remained hidden for centuries. It was exposed to view by coincidence in 1956. It was given the name of the "Hidden Church" by the people in the region because it remained hidden for centuries.

The fact that the frescoes within the church are still preserving their original condition is stemming from its remaining hidden.

THE KARANLIK (DARK) CHURCH

It is one of the domed churches constructed upon four columns. There is one large and on the sides are two small apses. It is one of the most beautiful churches constructed in the thirteenth century. The reason the paintings are lively and the paints have not faded is due to the fact that they did not get much sunlight from outside. There is a small window which opens outside. It was called the Karanlık (Dark) Church as very little light enters from here and the fact that it is a dimly lighted church.

The subjects in the Bible were transferred very beautifully onto the walls of this church as paintings. Among the frescoes of interest in the dome are the paintings of the consecration of Jesus, the Last Supper, the presentation of gifts to Jesus from the Three Kings, the assistance to sinful people, the Baptism, the Crucifixion, the betrayal of Judas, one of the disciples, the Gospel writers St. Mark and St. John and the apostles.

The Crucifixion of Jesus Christ.

The escape of Jesus Christ to Egypt together with those surrounding him and the Last Supper.

Jesus Christ's saving of the slaves fit for hell. It is related that the person whom He is holding by the hand is Anastasis.

Lazarus' risting fron the dead. The Angel Myrerophores and the women are in front of the empty tomb.

THE EL NAZAR CHURCH

On the Avcılar-Göreme highway, before reaching the Open-Air Museum, the El Nazar Church, that has remained alone among the vineyards, is reached after going for one kilometer the length the dry stream bed on the right, and advancing 100 meters more on the path that divides to the left and goes straight up. A portion of it was destroyed and despite the fact that for many years it has encountered considerable damage, the El Nazar Church has succeeded in remaining standing.

The paintings within this church, which is the symbol of Göreme, are frescoes belonging to the eleventh century. There are many paintings that are symbolizing Jesus's youth and life. Originally this church was two-storied and portions of the lower and upper stories were destroyed.

Today the restoration activities are being carried out by the Nevşehir Museum Directorate.

THE ELMALI (APPLE) CHURCH

When going to the region of churches, after passing the Nunnery the rock on the right side of the road has been hollowed out. A dome was placed on four columns. There is one large apse and there are two small apses. Even if the frescoes belonging to the Iconoclastic period were able to remain in good condition, the smashing and breaking from place to place is conspicuous on some of them. Within the dome is Jesus's consecration, while on the walls are paintings symbolizing the Baptism, the Last Supper before the migration to Jerusalem, the Crucifixion and the betrayal of Judas, one of the disciples.

The name of Elmalı (Apple) Church was given because in one of the paintings on the wall the round shape in Jesus's hand resembles an apple. In reality, according to some researchers, this symbolizes the world.

On the right and left portions of the arch found in the middle of the church is Daniel in the right corner and the Prophet Elijah in the left corner with opened scrolls in their hands.

THE YILANLI (SNAKE) CHURCH

The Yılanlı (Snake) Church is one of the churches of interest at Göreme. There are no columns or domes at this church. It has a curved ceiling and the paintings were made on the side. There is also a tomb within the church. It is observed that Constantine and Helen are holding the Cross with their left hands on the left wall at the entrance. Next to it is a painting showing the struggle of St. George and St. Theodore with a snake.

On the right side are paintings of St. Basil, St. Thomas and Onouphrios. According to hearsay, previously Onouphrios was a woman of light disposition. She was tired of men bothering her to an excessive degree and she prayed to God to save her. God accepted her prayer and had whiskers grow on her face and made her ugly. She is in the state of half man and half woman because of this.

Constantine and Helen who provided great services to Christianity. Onouphrios when she was a woman, became half man and half woman. St. George and St. Theodore on horseback struggling with the dragon.

THE TOKALI (BUCKLED) CHURCH

The group of structures called the Tokalı (Buckled) Church is the largest known rock church in the region and is composed of four structures. These are the small dimensioned single nave old church, the church below the old church, the large new church and the side chapel to the north of the old church.

Although the Old Church is in the form of the entrance to the New Church today, originally it was a single naved, cradle vaulted structure. During the additions at the eastern part of the New Church, the apse was completely torn down and it was decorated with a cycle containing the life of Jesus. The scenes have been placed on the surfaces of the vault and on the upper portion of the walls. It has been dated as being from around the beginning of the tenth century.

The cycle containing Jesus Christ's life has been separated into panels on the vault at the entrance and the scenes on the panels start at the right wing and follow each other directly towards the left wing. On the upper panel of the right wing of

The group of structures called the Tokalı (Buckled) Church is the largest known rock church in the region and is composed of four structures. These are the small dimensioned single nave old church, the church below the old church, the large new church and the side chapel to the north of the old church.

Although the Old Church is in the form of the entrance to the New Church today, originally it was a single naved, cradle vaulted structure. During the additions at the eastern part of the New Church, the apse was completely torn down and it was decorated with a cycle containing the life of Jesus. The scenes have been placed on the surfaces of the vault and on the upper portion of the walls. It has been dated as being from around the beginning of the tenth century.

The cycle containing Jesus Christ's life has been separated into panels on the vault at the entrance and the scenes on the panels start at the right wing and follow each other directly towards the left wing. On the upper panel of the right wing of the vault are the Joyful Tidings, the Visitation, the proof of Virginity, the journey to Bethlehem, the Nativity; on the upper panel of the left wing the homage of the three wise men, the massacre of the innocent children, the escape to Egypt, Jesus Christ's offering at the place of worship, the murdering of Zachariah; on the middle panel of the right wing the pursuing of Elizabeth, John the Baptist's call to repentence, John the Baptist's predictions, the meeting of Jesus Christ with John the Baptist, the Baptism, the Passover; on the middle panel of the left wing the Miracle of the Wine, the multiplication of the bread and fish, the appointing of the Disciples; on the lower panel of the right wing the entrance into Jerusalem, the Last Supper, the Betrayal, Jesus Christ before Pontius Pilate; on the lower panel of the left wing Jesus Christ on the road to Gethsemane, Jesus Christ on the Cross, Jesus Christ's descent from the Cross, the burial of Jesus Christ, the women in front of the empty tomb, the Resurrection of Jesus Christ and the Ascension of Jesus Christ. The holy scriptures are on the bottom of this panel while on top of the entrance is the scene of the transfiguration.

The New Church has a transverse rectangular plan; simple vaults, with a longitudinal narthex and a transverse nave. On the eastern wall are 4 columns connected to each other by arches and behind the columns is a raised corridor and after the corridor are located a large apse and two small and one side apse. To the left of the entrance is a small side apse separated by columns. At the cradle vaulted narthex the Jesus cycle has been worked according to chronological period by using mostly red and blue colors. The dark blue color is the most important characteristic that distinguishes the Tokalı Church from the others.

At the transverse nave are located scenes belonging mostly to Jesus Christ's miracles, the scriptures of the saints and St. Basil's life. The church has been dated as being from the end of the tenth century or the beginning of the eleventh century.

The scenes: the Joyful Tidings, the Visitation, Joseph's accusation of the Virgin Mary, the proof of her Virginity, the journey to Bethlehem, Joseph's dream, the Nativity, the homage of the three wise men, the escape to Egypt, Jesus Christ's offering at the place of worship, Jesus Christ among the

THE CARIKLI CHURCH

The Carıklı Church is at the end of the chain of churches of the Göreme Open Air Museum. Its stone stairs have been damaged by erosion and access to the church is through iron stairs made later.

It has three abscissas and 4 domes. Its frescos are very similar to those of the Karanlık (dark) and El-malı Churches. The paintings, of the Karanlık Church too have been made of the some period, at the beginning of the 13 th century. As in other churches, the paintings of the Carıklı Church depict scenes such as the cracification of Jesus, the taking of Jesus from the cross, the resuscitation of Lazarus, women at the empty tomb, the hospitality of the Prophet Abraham, Mary and the childhood of Jesus, the metamorphosis, the entry of Jesus into Jerusalem.

WINTER AT CAPPADOCIA

In general snow starts to fall at Cappadocia in December and January. The temperature falls to minus 15°C on days when it is severe and there are blizzards. Sometimes the depth of the snow reaches 35-40 centimeters.

As can be seen in the photographs, the snow covers one side of the fairy chimneys and the valleys and the other portions are remaining clear. The fairy chimneys and the valleys that are wrapped in a blanket of snow in this season display a vista that has never been seen before.

ORTAHİSAR

Ortahisar is a small town connected to Ürgüp which was founded one kilometer to the south on the Nevşehir-Ürgüp road. The biggest feature of Ortahisar is that it has a citadel like that at Uçhisar. The citadel was used at the time of the Christians as a shelter. It is possible to see the Göreme Valley from the top of the citadel. In the town are churches which are called the Üzümlü (Grape) Church, the Harun Church, and the Sarıca Church.

Other than these, there are hundreds of citrus fruit storehouses at Ortahisar. A portion of these were built at the time of the Christians and after being restored by the Turks, they are being used today as well. The citrus fruits, that are stored here for a specific period of time, are later shipped to various locations in the country.

Carpet weaving, viniculture, viticulture and selling of wines are the main sources of income for the people.

UÇHİSAR

Uçhisar is a touristic town in Nevşehir Province on the Nevşehir-Ürgüp highway at a distance of eight kilometers from Nevşehir and twelve kilometers from Ürgüp and one kilometer to the left off the main highway. The village houses were first of all built surrounding the citadel, but with an increase in population and because of erosion, they have descended as far as the lower parts of the town. Because of this, the citadel has remained completely within the town. There is an old hollowed out cave within the citadel. The cave can be entered by three separate paths and these paths meet at a spacious room. At one of the paths is a stone door and immediately after that is a watchman's room. Besides these, three rooms and storage depots are prominent. There are other long, narrow corridors within the citadel, but some of these have collapsed and some are filled with stones and soil.

The greatest feature of Uçhisar is that from the citadel the entire Göreme Valley is seen. Because of this, it is most suitable for those who have a great interest in taking photographs. The home pensions at Uçhisar, that have recently started operating, are popular because the Turkish and foreign tourists who are staying at Uçhisar are able to find the opportunity to watch comfortably the Göreme Valley, the fairy chimneys and the surroundings from the garden or the window of the room at the pension where they stay.

ÇAVUŞİN

One arrives at Çavuşin village after following the Nevşehir-Ürgüp highway for three to four kilometers and by taking the Uçhisar road on the left for another ten kilometers. This village is famous for the houses and churches of the Christian clergymen. In general the churches were constructed between the first and tenth centuries C.E.

Some of the churches are located at Güllüdere and Kızılcıklar and are used by the local people as "pigeon houses". One of the most important and interesting locations is a "Basilica" type church that was made by hollowing out the rocks at the edge of a precipice.

This church was made for St. John. Despite the wearing away at the front part as a result of erosion, the decorated pillar within the church has remained up until today.

There is another church that is called the "Pigeon House" in the direction of the exit from Avanos village. The front part of this, just like the other church, has become destroyed as a result of erosion and some of the frescoes have remained buried. One can ascend with an iron staircase constructed later on the destroyed front to the actual church section where there are many more frescoes. At this church there are no supporting columns and the ceiling is in the form of a half crescent. In the middle is one large hollow and on the sides are two small hollows. At this church mostly Jesus's life and the words of the Gospel are represented. In general brown and green colors are used in the frescoes.

There is a monastery right next to the church and four tombs that have been added within it.

PAŞA BAĞLARI

It is situated a distance of 1 km. the road turning toward the Zelve ruins in the Göreme-Avanos direction. Paşa Bağları is being visited by a large number of local and foreign tourists since it is the highest place in the region and has multi-head fairy chimneys.

In the region in question Paşa Bağları and Aşk Vadisi are among the places with very different and high fairy chimneys. Aşk Vadisi is a 4 km. long valley at the north of the Avcılar town. It is called Aşk Vadisi (the Valley of Love) because of its many fairy chimneys springing up from the soil and its silence broken only by the chirruping of birds.

In Paşa Bağları there is a hallowed out three-head fairy chimney with two rooms inside it. One of the rooms has been used as seclusion room by the 5th century monk St. Simeon. This place is called Paşa Bağları (Pasha's Vineyards) because someone called Pasha had vineyards where the fairy chimneys are situated.

GÜLŞEHİR AND AÇIKSARAY

Gülşehir was established twenty kilometers to the northwest of Nevşehir right next to a bend in the Kızılırmak River and at the foot of the Kepez Hill. It was first founded before Christ by the Hittites with the name of Zoropassos and it is thought that the Greeks later changed this name to "Arıbusun". After the forming of the Republic of Turkey the name of this town became Gülşehir. Today it is a county in Nevşehir Province.

When one has gone two kilometers from Gülşehir directly towards Nevşehir, one comes upon the first Christian shelters, that are known as Açıksaray, where hundreds of rock cavities have been hollowed out in the form of half valleys. It is worth seeing the paintings here from the sixth and seventh centuries C.E., even if they have been partial-ly destroyed. The St. Jean Church is in the same location and a tunnel approximately 100 meters long connects the two valleys to each other.

There are underground cities located at the villages of Sığırlı, Gümüşkent, Sivasa and Göstesin which are connected to Gülşehir, that have not been opened to the public. Furthermore, there are hieroglyphic inscriptions at Sivasa Village, once again belonging to the Hittites, that have been worked in the sides of the rocks. It does not stop with this at Sivasa; to the west there is a Byzantine church hollowed out of the rocks. However, the frescoes within the church which are symbolizing Jesus, the Virgin Mary and many saints have been partially destroyed.

ZELVE

While looking at different types of interesting fairy chimneys, one arrives at the former village of Zelve, that is a tourist attraction, three kilometers after turning to the right on the Göreme-Avanos road.

Here it is possible to see the most beautiful and different fairy chimneys in the Cappadocia Region. In particular, the fairy chimneys in the Paşabağ region are very interesting. The fairy chimneys here are in groups and their heights are changing between 15 to 20 meters and some of them have three tips.

There is a church and a monastery remaining from the Iconoclastic period at the former village of Zelve. The caves here were used as places of hiding at the time of the Christians.

Just as in some of the towns and villages, there are signs at the former village of Zelve showing that the Moslems and Christians lived together here. A structure that resembles an old mosque minaret has remained in good condition. After Zelve was abandoned by the Christians, it was used for housing by the Turks as well for a period of time. In 1950 it was also abandoned by the Turks because of erosion that was experienced here a number of times, and a new village was established somewhat further on from here and the village people moved there. Later, the former village of Zelve was opened to tourism and made into a museum and has become a place visited and liked by Turkish and foreign tourists.

ÜRGÜP (OSIANA)

Ürgüp (Osiana) is on the road to Kayseri, twenty kilometers to the east of Nevşehir and at a distance of seven kilometers from Göreme. The altitude is 1800 meters. Ürgüp was founded at the foot of the Temenni Hill and it is seen on some maps from ancient times that its name was Osiana. Ürgüp is one of the richest counties in Nevşehir Province from all aspects. Ürgüp was known in the world before Nevşehir from the point of view of historical and natural beauties.

As a result of the activities undertaken by Ali Baran Numan-oğlu, one of the former mayors, and with the cooperation of the people, they are constructing hotels, campgrounds, pensions, discotheques and places of entertainment for the Turkish and foreign tourists. Turkish hospitality is displayed to the tourists with the activities organized here.

At Ürgüp there are historical works such as a caravanserai, Turkish bath, fountain, mosque and library belonging to the Seljuk and Ottoman periods.

The tomb of one of the Seljuk sovereigns, Kılıçaslan, is on the Temenni Hill, which is Ürgüp's highest hill. In 1963, one of the citizens of Ürgüp, Mustafa Güzelgöz was given an award by President John F. Kennedy, because he established the first traveling library service by donkey and in 1969 in Amsterdam, he was chosen as the Librarian of the Year. Ürgüp's wines, handicrafts, kilims and woven carpets are as famous as their historical monuments and natural beauties and an international wine festival is held every year in October.

It is possible to watch the most beautiful sunsets in the region at Kızılçukur, three kilometers to the west of Ürgüp.

MUSTAFA PAŞA (SINOSON, SINOSOS)

Mustafa Paşa is a town established within the Mustafa Paşa Valley some five kilometers to the south of Ürgüp. It is one of the places which is drawing the attention of the Turkish and foreign tourists coming to this area because of the very different structures of the village houses.

The first things attracting attention when one enters the town are the methods of construction of the houses and the decorations on the edges of the doors and windows.

The Greek Christians were living here prior to the population exchanges between Turkey and Greece which followed the signing of the Treaty of Lausanne in 1923. However, after the exchange, the Turks settled here.

The names Sinoson and Sinosos were given to this town by the Greeks and was changed to Mustafa Paşa by the Turks.

In the town is a two story monastery remaining from the Greeks which is now used as a touristic hotel, but the frescoes in the interior have remained in good condition. There is the Aypos Vasilios Church at a distance of one kilometer from the village. This church is only one story and one walks down on carved stone steps. The church was completely hollowed out from within the rock and was placed on four columns. The frescoes in the interior are of interest although the church does not have much of a history.

A group of women who are celebrating at Anatolian weddings.

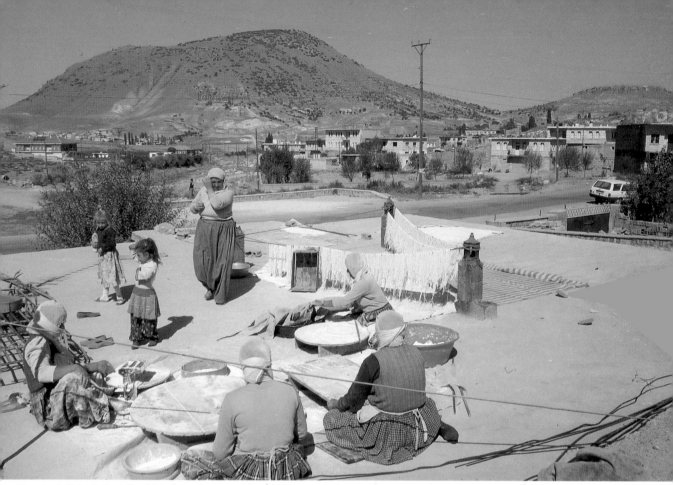

The people living in Anatolia obtain their winter provisions in the summertime. In the photograph are shown women who are making macaroni.

THE UNDERGROUND CITIES AND THE PEOPLE WHO MADE THEM

It is without a doubt that among the locations attracting the attention of visitors who come to Cappadocia, the underground cities have been first in importance. With the cooperation formed by nature, history and human beings, Cappadocia has historical and natural beauties whose equal has not yet been encountered in any other location in the world.

There are thirty-six underground cities in this region. I believe that in the future it will increase even more with new findings. Who can know in how many years the construction of all these underground cities was completed, how many thousands of people worked on building them, how they were able to realize these magnificent works with the techniques in former times and how the excavations of soil removed from the underground cities were transported to the surface and how they were eliminated? In fact, everything can be done or accomplished with human labor and strength. However, it would not be easy to accomplish these with the techniques at that time.

The most suitable method that occurs to one for briefly explaining how to construct the underground cities is, first of all, the hollowing out of air shafts that descend as far as water and that are at depths reaching 70 to 85 meters; later, the building of the underground cities, by making excavations directly towards the sides from the shafts and the extraction of the excavations of soil by means of a pulley wheel from the air shafts which have been previously opened. If they did not previously open the air shafts, then they would not work comfortably from lack of air and they would not have produced these magnificent works of art.

This question comes to mind immediately while explaining briefly the excavation of the underground cities. Where did they dump these excavations of earth dug out from the underground cities and how was it eliminated? Certainly, the excavations of soil removed from an underground city, that reaches a depth of 70 to 85 meters in some areas and that covers an area of 4 km2, should form a large hill.

It is possible to give an answer to this question in this manner. The Cappadocia Region is a hilly location with abundant valleys, if it is considered from the point of view of the morphology. The excavations of soil from the underground cities were dumped into suitable streams in the area and were

lost in time by undergoing erosion. The surroundings of Derinkuyu form a flat area. However, inside the excavation center there is a stream that comes from the direction of Kaymaklı-Derinkuyu. This stream, that has a width of approximately 50 to 60 meters and a length of eight kilometers, is now completely filled. I am of the opinion that a portion of the excavations of soil extracted from the underground city were dumped into this stream and a portion were dumped at the foot of the Söğdele Hill on the western front of Derinkuyu. The excavations of soil extracted would have produced a large hill if they had been heaped in another location. Whereas, there is not such a heaped hill in this region. If it is conjectured that the excavations of soil extracted were spread over the land, then there would be a soil with lime and it would be arid and not produce crops in the region where the excavations of soil were dumped. Nevertheless there is not such an

area. This region has a completely productive agricultural land.

In fact, it was not too hard to hollow out the underground cities, which are located among the volcanic tufa and lava of Erciyes Mountain in the east and Hasan Mountain in the west. In general, the underground cities were excavated in locations in the regions where volcanic tufa was found. In fact, they are not as hard as they seem and the places excavated, when they are in contact with air, are becoming hard in time. In any case, if they had not been soft, then they would not have been able to produce these underground cities with the techniques used at that time.

If one pays attention, the differences are conspicuous between the first stories and the last stories and some of the air shafts at some of the underground cities. The upper stories and some of the air shafts have become more hardened in comparison with the others. It was seen that they have been made haphazardly and that no chisel was used while they were being made. The lower stories and some of the air shafts are softer and have not become very hardened and some places can still be excavated easily while the chisel marks are very obvious in the excavated places. However, it is not becoming hardened in a short period of

time and the marks are not disappearing in the excavated places. In particular, it is necessary for a long period of time to pass for the chisel marks to disappear. This means that there was quite a time difference between the years of construction of the first stories and the last stories at the underground cities. In 1910 the Englishman R. Campbell Thomson found things like stones and a hand ax belonging to the Paleolithic Age in the Soğanlı Stream at a distance of twenty-six kilometers from Derinkuyu. In any case, as there are also underground cities in this region, I wonder whether these cities are belonging to the Paleolithic Age? It is still not known, because up until now, no archaeological excavation or study has been undertaken in this region. However, definite evidence that the Romans and Byzantines were living here is the finding of a church in the shape of a cross on the seventh story of the Derinkuyu underground city and later on the making of a missionary school and a place of baptism by improving even more the first stories.

The ventilation systems of the underground cities were made in an organized manner. It is such that there is a very clean air circulation as one descends to the lower floors. In particular, the fact that it has been cleaned up until the last floors at

the Derinkuyu Underground city, plays a great role in being aware of the air circulation. It is seen that cigarette smoke is drawn up directly in a rapid manner when one approaches the air shaft at the seventh story. In these sections the temperature is around 7° to 8°C and is not changing in summer or winter. In distant locations from the air shafts the temperature is between 13° to 15°C. The holes with a diameter of approximately ten centimeters and a length of three to four meters which are opening from the first floor of the city to the ground surface are one of the locations at the underground cities which is attracting attention. It is conjectured that these holes were used as a communication system and were perforated with a wooden drill with metal points. Double holes next to each other in some places are conspicuous while in other places single holes are prominent.

Up until the present only some of the sections of the underground cities have been opened to the public. We do not have very much information concerning these cities. We are constantly confronted with questions because of this. For example, questions are gradually increasing concerning how these underground city people were living with a crowded population.

Very few kitchens are encountered in these underground cities which we have seen and visited.

However, it is necessary for there to be a kitchen for every family or one to two families. We are seeing that many families were using a kitchen in common. The fact that the people were forced to make few fires to be able to continue their lives is the reason for this, because it was thought that with the use of many kitchens at the same time, the smoke coming from these would draw attention to these cities and that there was the chance of being discovered easily by their enemies. The need arose for making few kitchens because of this.

Still, even if some holes were found that resembled toilets at these underground cities, they have not gained a certitude. Only the toilets at the underground cities of Tatlarin and Gelveri are definite and made extremely regularly and are even in a condition in which they could be used today. The underground cities of Tatlarin and Gelveri are on the slope of a hill. There is even the septic pit of their toilets. These are underground cities from the Byzantine period. Villages have been established on top of some of the underground cities, while there is nothing on top of some of them. Moreover, the foundation stones are not even encountered. I wonder how the people were taking care of their toilet needs at the underground cities established on this flat land? This need would be eliminated in normal times by going outside. At the times when they encountered an invasion, the people stuck inside would use things like earthenware pots and pans and so that they did not make a smell or produce illness, they would cover the top of it with sand and would take it outside at a suitable time. This must be the most suitable method.

No clues concerning the wearing apparel of these people have been encountered to date during the cleaning up of the underground cities that have been opened to the public for tourism. The underground cities are somewhat chilly, and it would have been necessary for them to use different clothing because of this. It can be thought that they used woolen animal hides during the times when they stayed below.

In addition, let's consider how tall were these people. The corridors of all the underground cities are at a height of between 160 to 170 cm. It is not certain whether these people were short or tall.

It is certain that great importance was placed on animals and wines in those times, because a good many stables and wineries are found on the first floors of all the underground cities.

These people about whom we are talking sewed and planted their lands without difficulty. Moreover, they had productive soil at the foot of hills and were able to use these places without problems, despite the fact that they were distant from the cities. How were they able to protect themselves and how were they able to communicate when an enemy attacked?

There are many more hills and small mountains at Cappadocia such as Erdaş, Karadağ, Çağnı and Kahveci Mountains. On top of some of these hills and mountains there were sentry boxes and in time one sees that these disappeared and only the foundation stones remained. They were able to ensure communication from these sentry boxes by reflecting mirrors to each other.

These underground cities had a very significant

role in the first spreading of Christianity. This situation is understood from some of the articles found during the cleaning of these underground cities, such as old coins, pots and pans and oil lamps which were used as a means of illumination. The underground cities were not used after the eighth century C.E.

The underground cities remained empty for centuries and filled with snow, rain, rocks and soil from the doors and the air shafts. Some places were partially closed and some places were completely closed. Because of this, villages and towns were established on top of some of them, without being aware of the portions underneath.

The round stone doors are one of the aspects of the underground cities which are arousing the most interest. The thicknesses of these are between 55 to 65 cm and their heights are 170 to 175 cm and their weights are between 300 to 500 kg and the degree of hardness of the rocks from the underground cities and the stones from the rocks excavated are not conforming to each other. For this reason, these were not made below, but were made above, that is on the ground, and were brought down below.

In general, all the places of settlement of the underground cities, either opened or not opened to the public to date, have been directly in eastern, southern and western directions to the hills.

The fact that the winters are very cold and with snow in this region is the reason why they were not established on the northern side.

No one can answer definitely the questions concerning who were the first persons to make the underground cities, in which century they started to make them, where these tribes had come from and why they felt the need to build these cities.

THE DERİNKUYU UNDERGROUND CITY (Melegüp, Melegopia)

Derinkuyu is on the Nevşehir-Niğde highway and is a county of Nevşehir Province with a population of 7,000 according to the 1986 Population Census. The elevation is 1355 meters and it is at a distance of twenty-nine kilometers from Nevşehir, the provincial center, and fifty kilometers from Niğde. Derinkuyu is an Anatolian town that has recently started to be known and has become a place, with its underground city, its above ground churches, its hospital for mental diseases and its historical richness, where thousands of tourists visit every day.

The underground city was found by chance and was opened to the public in 1965 by the General Directorate of Antiquities and Museums. The visitors have arrived at the consensus that it is the ninth wonder of the world and it is conjectured that the Hittites, Romans and Byzantines lived here and moreover that even the Proto-Hittites lived here. On the other hand, it is supposed that the first stories were made and used by the Proto-Hittites as a storehouse and that the eight story underground city of today was enlarged with additions made by other peoples who came later.

There are thirty-six more underground cities in the Cappadocia Region and for the first people who believed in Christianity, the underground cities were safe locations both to spread their religion secretly and to carry out their religious obligations far from all kinds of pressure and later on they were used as a shelter against the Arab raids that started in the sixth and seventh centuries C.E. There are the missionary school, the place of baptism, the kitchen, the storeroom, the bedrooms, the dining rooms, the wine cellars and the stables on the first and second stories. There are the places of hiding, the storehouses for weapons and the tunnels on the third and fourth stories. They would save themselves by escaping through these tunnels when the city encountered a large attack. It is surmised that a tunnel found on the third story is connected to the Kaymaklı underground city at a distance of nine kilometers. As the ventilation shafts of the tunnel are within the farmland, they were not kept intact, filled with rocks and soil and were destroyed in some locations.

It is apparent from some traces which are displayed that the other stories of the underground city were a shelter. One of these are the stone doors in the corridors (Tırhıs). The people were descending to the shelters below and the corridors were closed with these bolt stones at the times when the city was raided. It was not possible to open these stone doors from outside. They could

only be opened and closed from inside. There is a hole in the center. These holes were to defend themselves from any kind of attack from outside. There are special water wells, hidden desertion shafts, a church, a conference room, a place of confession, a tomb and ventilation shafts on the final stories.

There are fifty-two more ventilation shafts within Derinkuyu. The depth of these is varying between 70 to 85 meters, as the city is on a somewhat sloped surface. The bottom portion of these are water wells and the top portion are ventilation shafts and all the floors are able to obtain air from these. In any case, the city got its name from these wells and the former name was Melegopia.

The water needs of Derinkuyu County were obtained from these wells by means of pulley wheels up until 1962.

The width of the church on the last story is ten meters, the length is twenty-five meters and the height is two and one half meters. The structure is in the form of a cross. There is a conference room with three columns exactly opposite this church. A tomb was found at the end of a corridor on the right side of the conference room when the underground city was cleaned up. It is empty at the moment. It is reported that a skeleton which was found within the tomb was sent to Ankara for analysis. There are 450 to 500 more underground cities like this underground city opened to the public beneath Derinkuyu. There are 600 descent and ascent doors belonging to these. Some of the sections of the first floors of the underground cities are used by the people as a storehouse as some of these doors are within houses which are still being occupied. It is difficult to walk around in them because the floors at deeper levels are partially filled with soil. There are locations which are descending for eighteen to twenty stories beneath some of the houses. It is estimated that a portion of the soil removed from the underground city, which covers a 4 km^2 area and was calculated as able to shelter 2,000 households, was dumped at the foot of the Söğdele Hill to the west of Derinkuyu and a portion was dumped within the dried up stream in the direction of Kaymaklı-Derinkuyu.

If it is considered that an average of 10,000 persons could live at the underground city, it can be better understood as to what people's labor and strength sufficed within the possibilities at that time. At the moment whatever sort of a city there is above, there is a city with a history below.

Exactly 100,000 laborers worked for thirty years by the forced labor method in order to build the Egyptian pyramids. I wonder how many thousands of laborers worked hard for how many years and how many lives were lost in order to build the Derinkuyu underground city?

The answer to this question still has not been provided.

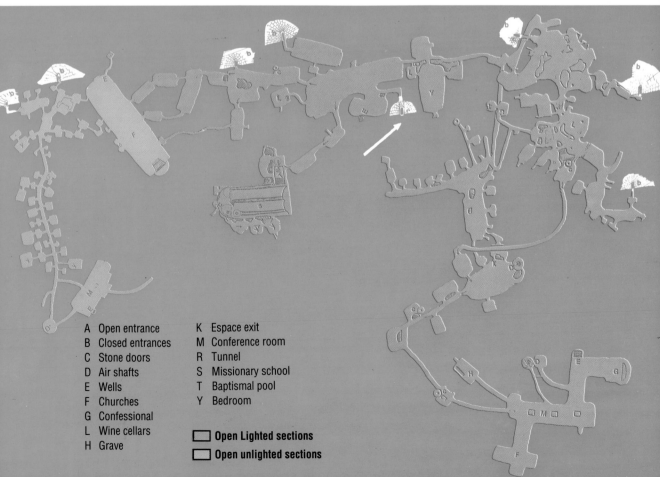

A	Open entrance	K	Espace exit
B	Closed entrances	M	Conference room
C	Stone doors	R	Tunnel
D	Air shafts	S	Missionary school
E	Wells	T	Baptismal pool
F	Churches	Y	Bedroom
G	Confessional		
L	Wine cellars		
H	Grave		

▭ **Open Lighted sections**

▭ **Open unlighted sections**

1- ENTRANCE
2- CLOSED ENTRANCE
3- CANAL
4- AIR VENTS
5- CHURCH
6- STONE DOORS

The Plan of the

Underground City.

KAYMAKLI (Enegüp, Soandus)

This town was established on the highway between Niğde and Nevşehir at a distance of twenty kilometers from Nevşehir and nine kilometers from Derinkuyu. Although the founding date of the town is not definite, the former name was Enegüp and before the population exchanges it was called Enegobi by the Greeks living here and was changed to Kaymaklı by the Turks. Enegüp (Kaymaklı), Melegüp (Derinkuyu) and Güple were former neighboring settlement centers established on the same route. The name of this place is recorded as Soandus on some maps.

An underground city located under a hill was found in 1964 in the middle of the town that is called by the name of Kaymaklı today and was opened to tourism. In spite of the fact that the places that can be visited are four stories, it has still not been determined how many stories there are, together with the unilluminated portions.

One can walk in a flat area, without descending too far down, after a descent of approximately fifteen to twenty meters.

This city, as with the other cities, had been carved by the people who had accepted Christianity and who escaped with the fear of oppression and extinction and were used against their enemies both as a shelter and as a safe place to carry out their worship.

Even if it appears as though the city was constructed in a disorganized manner, it is evident in the excavations that a great care and skill were shown because in spite of the fact that the tunnels and rooms are so confused, one room excavated did not collide with another room and were not connected to each other.

Conspicuous among the places to visit are the bedrooms, the food storehouses, the wine cellars,

the ventilation shafts, the water reservoirs, the church with double apses for worship and the stone doors for protecting against all kinds of dangers which could come from outside. These stone doors, just as at the other underground cities, were placed in the tunnels here as well and could only be opened and closed from the interior portions.

There are simply made graves on the rocks exactly on top of the underground city and these have been completely cleaned out.

Carved tombs whose insides are empty, just like the tombs on top of the hill, are found in a room on the second story of the underground city. One ventilation shaft and one kitchen are encountered in the places that are open and visited at the Kaymaklı underground city, that has many rooms and is no different from an ant hill. It has still not been determined how many or where the other ventilation shafts and kitchens are located.

The stone doors which are used to close the corridors have thicknesses of 55 to 60 cm and heights of 170 to 175 cm. The weight is over 500 kg. Just as with the other underground cities, excluding Özkonak, the stone doors of this underground city also came from outside, because the degree of hardness of the underground cities and the degree of hardness of the stone doors are inconsistent with each other. The degree of hardness of the underground city is between 14 to 18, while the degree of hardness of the stone doors is between 30 to 35. For this reason, it is understood that these stone doors were brought from outside, and were not made inside. They were not brought from the route visited today, but were brought from the location next to it that is covered with rocks. The Kaymaklı underground city is one of the underground cities which is worth seeing.

Cross-section of the Kaymaklı Underground City.

MAZI KÖYÜ (Mataza)

Mazı village is one of the locations in the Cappadocia Region in which tourism has not been promoted and brought to light. If one follows an eastern direction seven-eight kilometers from Kaymaklı, one reaches the village that is established in a streambed.

The places of interest here are consisting of the old tombs carved in the high rocks, chapels and churches with various structures and the underground city. Tombs were made in three different forms. Four of these have columns and are drawing great attention. Although some of the tombs are without columns, the interior portions where the corpse was placed are the same. The total number of columned and uncolumned tombs is approximately thirty. The other tombs that are made on the flat area on top of the rocks are numbering in the thousands.

Even though there are a great number of churches and chapels on the rocks above the village and in the region of the Bağırsak Stream, some of these have been destroyed or filled with soil. However, a carved church has remained in good condition within the rocks to the south of the village. This church was constructed with a column in the center, a large apse on the left hand side of the entrance and a double-arched ceiling. One each large cross is conspicuous on both sides of the apses. There is also the same cross on the front surface of the column in the center, while a motif has been worked by connecting small crosses to each other on the broad surface facing the north.

The underground city within the village is entered from a rock cavity from the east to the west. It is not definite where the real entrance door is located because in time the high rocks broke off from their places and the real entrance door disappeared. In spite of the fact that the falling rocks opened new entrance doors, the entrances opened are at great heights.

It is hard to determine the stories of the underground city which is still difficult to visit because it has collapsed in some places and has been filled with soil in other places.

In any case, Mazı village is one of the historical places which should be brought to light and promoted for tourism. At the moment it is in a state of ruin.

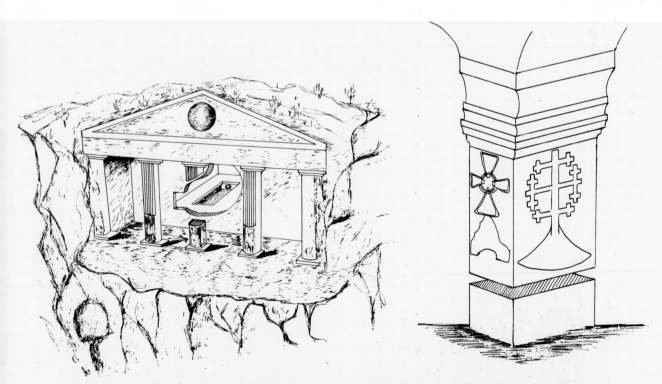

A columned tomb carved in the rocks on the left side of the entrance to the village and the column with crosses within the church.

AVANOS

The founding date of Avanos County, that is located at a distance of fifteen kilometers from Nevşehir Province, is not exactly known.

Evranos Bey, who migrated from the east to the west, settled to the south of Ziyaret Mountain, close to the Kızıl-ırmak River. The town remained within the boundaries of a Seljuk nomad tribe of which Evranos Bey was in command and first of all it was called Evranos and later this name became Avanos.

In antiquity the region was known as "Vanessa". Vanessa means "the city on the river" in Latin.

The first people who lived in Avanos were making ceramic articles, earthenware water jugs, plates, saucers, dishes, large earthenware jars and other household utensils.

Today the citizens of Avanos are continuing this tradition and they are known for their ceramic products.

Furthermore, carpet weaving and similar production activities are adding a distinctive harmony to the surroundings in this touristic center.

In addition, tourists are staying with great satisfaction and visiting with pleasure at Saruhan, Zelve, Çavuşin, Avcılar, Göreme and Özkonak, which are very close to Avanos.

ÖZKONAK

Özkonak lies twelve kilometers to the north of Avanos in the direction of Gülşehir. The "Yallı Damı Shelter" and the "Belha Monastery" are in the section right to the south of the town. This monastery is from the Byzantine period and is a typical example of the other monasteries found at Cappadocia.

The underground city was exposed to view in 1972 by the muezzin of the mosque, Latif Acar, while he was working in his garden. The activities for cleaning the underground city were made by the Özkonak Municipality and it was opened for tourism in 1973. Latif Acar undertook the protection of this underground city until 1990. The number of Turkish and foreign visitors coming to the underground city increased to a great extent and in 1990 the underground city, that was under the jurisdiction of the Museum Directorate, was transferred to the Private Administration Directorate.

There are places for feeding animals, granaries and wine cellars, just as with the other underground cities, and the stone doors are attracting attention.

In general, the stone doors were made outside and put inside at all the underground cities at Cappadocia. The thickness of the stone doors is 60 cm, the height is 170 cm and the weight is 500 kg. These stone doors were made inside the city and the places where they were made are still evident.

There is a stream that separates the town of Özkonak into three parts. The depth of the stream is thirty meters and the length is four kilometers. There is an old settlement place from end to end on the inner edges of this stream.

THE TATLARİN UNDERGROUND CITY AND THE ROCK CHURCHES

One arrives at the town of Tatlarin with a population of 3,500 after taking off at the twentieth kilometer on the Nevşehir-Aksaray road and by going nine kilometers directly to the north within Acıgöl County. The slopes of the Taşkale Hill to the east of the town were former settlement places and here there are rock churches and an underground city. The underground city was opened to the public in 1975. The fact that the toilets are very obvious here is a distinct feature.

Frescoes have been found in only two of the many rock churches and the upper surfaces of the frescoes have been covered with soot. The churches have been placed under the jurisdiction of the Nevşehir Museum Directorate and the restoration activities started in 1991.

KAYSERİ (Mazaca)

Kayseri is one of the crowded cities in the Central Anatolian Region. It has adjacent boundaries with Yozgat and Sivas in the north, Adana in the south, Kahramanmaraş in the east and Niğde and Nevşehir in the west.

If we take a glance at the history of Kayseri, whose former name was Mazaca, it is observed that it goes back to 2000 B.C. The baked clay tablets, the cuneiform writings, the letters and statues found at the remains in Kültepe, that lies twenty-two kilometers to the northeast of Kayseri, prove that Kayseri was an important Hittite city in the past. These items are the first works of art found in Anatolia and are preserved in the Kayseri and Kültepe Museums.

Kayseri was an important commercial city at the time of the Hittites and moreover, we understand from the written tablets that even the Assyrian merchants came here and traded. Other than the Hittites, Kayseri also experienced the rule of the Romans and Byzantines. Various monuments and temples were produced in Kayseri in the Roman period, in fact Kayseri had coins minted on behalf of the Roman king. These coins were usually bronze. They are found frequently. However, these temples and monuments in Kayseri were destroyed by the Byzantines with the development shown by Christianity in all of Cappadocia, along with the other regions.

Kayseri was frequently subjected to the invasions of various peoples after the Byzantines. Starting from A.D. 690, at the time when the Islamic religion started to spread, Kayseri encountered the invasions of the Arabs for short periods of time up until A.D. 726. Kayseri was occupied by the Seljuks after the Battle of Malazgirt in 1071, and later entered under the protection of Emir Gazi of the Danişmends and at the time of his son Melik Mehmet, it became the capital city of the beylic. However, one of the Seljuk Sultans, Kılıçaslan II recaptured Kayseri from the Danişmends in 1174 and Kayseri was furnished with the greatest development and restoration by these people. The majority of the works of art that have remained standing in Kayseri were belonging to the Seljuks, such as the Hunat Hatun Tomb, the Hunat Hatun

Mosque, the Hunat Hatun Madrasah Revolving Large Tomb, the Kılıçaslan Mosque, the Külük Mosque and the Kurşunlu Mosque. The Seljuks constructed khans, Turkish baths, madrasahs, caravanserais, fountains and mosques in other cities besides Kayseri and they decorated the interiors and exteriors of these with the Seljuk handcrafted works of art.

The Sultan Inn is the most beautiful work of art undertaken by the Seljuks at this period. It is at a distance of fifty kilometers from Kayseri on the Kayseri-Sivas road. The Sultan Inn was constructed at the time of Alâaddin Keykubat, during the period when the Seljuk works of art attained their zenith. The most beautiful decorations are on the entrance gate and the small mosque.

Later Kılıçaslan II divided the country among his sons and he took Konya and went into retirement. However, greed to possess the entire country occurred among his sons and a fight for the throne started among them. Moreover, they even marched on him.

In 1399 Kayseri was joined to the Ottomans by Yıldırım Beyazit, but after the Ankara War between Tamerlane and Yıldırım Beyazit, with the defeat of Yıldırım Beyazit, Tamerlane came all the way to Kayseri and utterly destroyed it. Even the Kayseri Citadel was leveled to the ground at this point.

Kayseri was later captured by the Dulkadiroğlus and the Karamanoğlus and the Karamanlıs repaired the Kayseri Citadel. Kayseri was once again joined to the Ottoman lands after the war between the Karaman Sovereign Pir Ahmet and the Ottoman Sovereign Fatih Sultan Mehmet Han, and even though it remained as a dilapidated city up until the Republic, after the forming of the Republic, great strides were made towards development in this city.

SOĞANLI (Sonakaldı, Soandos)

Soğanlı is located in a valley twenty-five kilometers to the east of Derinkuyu and at a distance of sixty-five kilometers to the northwest of Ürgüp. It was called "Soandos" at one time. However, according to a widespread tale, it is stated that it was the last place taken in the Arab invasions and it is described that after Battal Gazi took over many places in the region, he said that he left this place to the last for those coming from behind. In this way, its name became "Sonakaldı" (it was left to the last). This name changed for hundreds of years and today it became "Soğanlı" (lit. onion).

There are about 150 interesting churches, most of which are filled with soil, in the Soğanlı Valley, while the others have been transformed into pigeon houses. Of these churches, the Yılanlı (Snake) Church, the Saklı Church (Church of St. John), the Meryem Ana (Virgin Mary) Church, the Karanlık (Dark) Church, the Tokalı (Buckled) Church and the Kubbeli (Domed) Church can be visited. The Domed Church is definitely worth visiting.

Soğanlı is as interesting as Göreme with its own special features.

IHLARA

Ihlara is reached by following the road turning to the left for another forty kilometers after the fifty-eighth kilometer on the Nevşehir-Ankara highway. It is possible to go from Derinkuyu to Ihlara by a shorter road. This road goes directly from Derinkuyu to Ihlara and is at a distance of forty kilometers. The Ihlara Valley of today, that is approximately 150 meters deep, was formed with the erosion of the Melendiz Stream that has continued for hundreds of years. It is drawing the attention of thousands of visitors with its hundreds of churches and the natural beauties that caress the eyes.

In 1969 the mummy of a virgin girl was found in this valley. This mummy is now in the Niğde Museum. The Ihlara Stream stretches in the direction of Belisırma, Yaprakhisar and Selimiye. The most beautiful churches scattered along the length of the stream are:

1. The Yılanlı (Snake) Church,
2. The Ağaç Altı Church,
3. The Sümbüllü (Hyacinth) Church,
4. The Kırk Dam Altı Church,
5. The Bahattin Samanlığı. ???

THE YILANLI (SNAKE) CHURCH

It is in the form of a long cross and in the western portion there is an empty tomb. There are paintings on the same side that show the weighing of sins and good deeds by St. Michael.

The painting immediately to the right shows the entwining of the sinful people's bodies by snakes. In the dome are Jesus's and the angels paintings, and on the southeastern side there is the painting of the death of the Virgin Mary. Besides these there is the Last Supper of Jesus, and portraits of the Virgin Mary and the saints.

THE AĞAÇ ALTI CHURCH

It is in the form of a cross and is older in comparison with the other churches. However, the pictures have remained in good condition. There is Daniel between two lions on the wall opposite the door and there is a picture of a dragon on the ceiling.

THE SÜMBÜLLÜ (HYACINTH) CHURCH

This is also in the shape of a cross and the paintings were made around the fourteenth century.

THE KIRK DAM ALTI CHURCH

Some of the events mentioned in the Bible have been rendered here as paintings. The murderer of St. Zachariah is seen here.

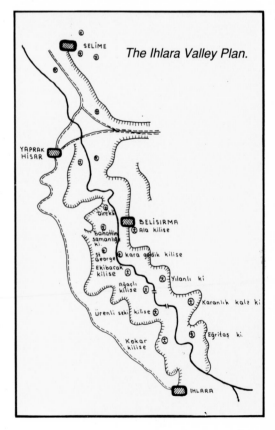

The Ihlara Valley Plan.

SELİME

YAPRAK HİSAR

Direkli
Sanattin
samanlık ki
St George
Ekibacak
kilise

BELİSIRMA
Ala kilise

kara gedik kilise

Ağaçlı
kilise

Yılanlı ki

Karanlık kale ki

Ürenli seki kilise

Eğritaş ki.

Kokar
kilise

IHLARA

NİĞDE (NAHITA)

Niğde is on the Adana-Kayseri highway and is a province within the southern boundary of the Cappadocia Region and the city is 500 meters to the west of the main highway. If we glance at the first history of Niğde, it is seen that it dates back to the Hittites, because in the Hittite hieroglyphic writing found in Andaval village in Niğde Province, it is understood that the Hittites called Niğde, Nahita. This hieroglyphic writing is now in the Museum of Anatolian Civilizations in Ankara. Besides this, in 1976 in Niğde a relief statue was found of one of the Hittite gods made of hard, black stone. Cuneiform writing is at the right hand edge of the stone, in the god's right hand is an ax, in the left hand the symbol of lightning, grapes at the left bottom and a sheaf of grain at the right bottom. This stone was found in a construction site close to the Kığlı Mosque and it was delivered to the Niğde Museum. After 710 B.C. Niğde came under Phrygian rule. In any case, this is corroborated by the Phrygian works of art found in the environs from time to time. After the Phrygians, the Romans lived as well in Niğde. However, not many works of art have been found belonging to them. In A.D. 53, the newly developing Christian religion started to advance rapidly, including this region as well. However, the heavy pressures and massacres by the Roman idol worshippers at Derinkuyu, Kırağcaşar, Belören, Kızılören and Til villages, just as it was the reason for the construction of the underground cities of Çekmi, Örentepe, Güble, Çakıllı, Doğala and Suvermez in Niğde, it was also the reason for the construction of the underground shelter cities of Gölcük, Misli, Tır-han, Hasanköy, Orhanlı and Edikli. I am of the opinion that there are close to one hundred underground cities in the Cappadocia Region other than these underground cities. The purpose of construction of these underground cities was both to protect themselves and to secretly spread the Christian religion. However, in A.D. 313 after the liberation of this religion by Emperor Constantine, they tried openly to spread their religion. Niğde was under the rule of the Byzantines from A.D. 395 to 1075 and from the beginning of the eleventh century to around the middle of the thirteenth century it became the residence of the Anatolian Seljuks. When one of the Seljuk Sultan's, Alâaddin Keykubat I ascended the throne, the Niğde Sancak Bey Zeyneddin Beşare had a mosque constructed here in the name of Alâaddin. The name of this mosque has remained as Alâaddin Mosque up until the present day. This mosque is still used today. The interior and exterior of the mosque are ornamented with stone decorations. The most important portions of the mosque are the *Mihrap* (niche in a mosque indicating the direction of Mecca) and the *Mimber* (pulpit beside the mihrap reached by a long, straight flight of stairs) and the main door that has a superb artistic value. Between 1219 to 1237, at the time when Alâaddin Keykubat was on the throne, the Anatolian Seljuk State experienced its most brilliant period. In all the cities where the Seljuk State ruled at this time, madrasahs, khans, Turkish baths, mosques, caravanserais and tombs were made and ornamented on the interior and exterior with their own handicrafts. However, after the death of Alâaddin, with the taking over of the state by Gıyaseddin Keyhüsrev II, the Anatolian Seljuk State started to become weak.

Iran and Caucasia were taken over by the Mongols at that date and it was a great danger for the Anatolian Seljuk State. The Mongols took advantage of the weakening of the Anatolian Seljuk State and entered Anatolia. The Seljuks were defeated in 1243 in the battle that occurred in the Kösedağ Region of Sivas and they started to pay taxes to the Mongols. Later the Seljuks accepted their rule. The Turkoman Beys, who were connected to the Seljuks, benefited from this situation and announced their independence here and there. After this, Niğde was occupied by peoples such as the İlhanlıs, the Karamanlıs and the Ottomans. Niğde, which was the home of peoples such as the Hittites, Phrygians, Romans, Byzantines, Seljuks, İlhanlıs, Karamanlıs and the Ottomans encountered invasions from time to time by the Sassanids and the Arabs. Thus, within these complicated events, there was a lot of destruction in Niğde, however, as the efforts required for development and restoration were not sufficient, Niğde started to regress completely. The touristic places to be seen in Niğde today are as follows:

1. The Alâaddin Mosque,
2. The Sungur Bey Mosque,
3. The Rahmaniye Mosque,
4. Large Domed Tombs,
5. The Ak Madrasah,
6. The Citadel.

ANCIENT GÜMÜŞ

There is a Byzantine monastery chiseled out of the rocks six kilometers to the northeast of Niğde. Rooms were built to the west and southeast of the courtyard in the front portion and the monastery was constructed in the north portion. The church is from around the tenth to eleventh centuries. A dome was placed on top of four large and round columns in the church. In the eastern portion there are three apses and in the north there is a room for praying. It is decorated with paintings of Jesus, the Virgin Mary and the saints. In another apse is a painting of the Virgin Mary with Jesus on her lap, symbolizing his childhood and it is a painting that is very lively and attracts attention.

There is an exit door descending directly underground at the southern part of the courtyard, but it is not possible to descend because the exit door is closed.

GÜZELYURT (KALVERİ, GELVERİ)

The town of Güzelyurt was founded in a valley at the northern foot of Hasan Mountain to the southwest of Cappadocia and is at a distance of fifteen kilometers from Ihlara and forty kilometers from Derinkuyu.

Although it was late in becoming known, it is understood from the Yüksek (High) Church and the ceramic remains found in the valley to the west of the town that the history of Güzelyurt dates back to very ancient times and that around 2500 B.C. it was one of the most important commercial centers.

The prehistoric age settlement here has not been spoiled and has lasted until the present day and the people are continuing their lives in proximity with past history.

According to some sources, it is stated that Gregorius, who made the calendar (Gregorian Calendar), which took the place of the Persian calendar that was used before Christ in Anatolia, was born in Nazianz (the name is Nenezi today) and the theologian Theologus was born in Kalveri (Güzelyurt today) and after this individual was proclaimed to be a saint, Kalveri became a religious center.

The prehistoric settlements remaining from before Christ, the rock churches and chapels after Christ, the Rock Mosque, the Büyük (Grand) Church and the Yüksek (High) Church are of great interest.

Ceramic making developed to such a great extent in Güzelyurt that despite all the time that has passed, the art of ceramic making has still continued up until the present. Among the ceramic pots made in the Cappadocia Region, the Gelveri pots are very famous.

On the Tilki (Fox) path and in the Pınarca location two underground tunnels were found which are still closed. While the residents of the village say that one of these tunnels is in the direction of the Ihlara Stream and the other goes directly to Hasan Mountain, it has still not become definite.

SELJUK HISTORY AND WORKS OF ART

The Turkish clans that started to come to Anatolia in large groups around the middle of the eleventh century joined together and founded the Anatolian Seljuk State. The Seljuks placed great importance on the arts of tile making and carpet making and stone working and they decorated every corner of Anatolia by constructing mosques, madrasahs, large tombs and caravanserais. In the twelfth century the Anatolian Seljuk works of art reached the summit of the art. Examples of these are the Konya Karatay Madrasah, the İnce Minareli (Fine Minareted) Madrasah, the Sivas Gök Madrasah and the Sivas Çifte Minareli (Double Minareted) Madrasah as well as many mosques, madrasahs and caravanserais.

The Seljuk works of art remaining within the boundaries of Cappadocia are the Alâaddin Mosque, the Hüdavent Hatun Large Tomb and the Sungur Bey Mosque in Niğde, the Honat Hatun Mosque and Madrasah, the Döner Vault in Kayseri, the Sultan Inn between Kayseri and Sivas, the Karatay Inn in Karaday village between Tomarza and Bünyan, the Sultan Inn between Aksaray and Konya, the Ağzıkara Inn and the Alay Inn between Nevşehir and Aksaray and the Sarı Inn located seven kilometers to the east of Avanos.

In the thirteenth century the Anatolian Seljuk State started to have major difficulties from the aspect of politics and administration. The Turkish Beylics such as the Germiyan-oğlus, Aydınoğlus, Menteş-oğlus and Karamanoğlus appeared in place of the Seljuk state that was collapsing.

The Ottoman Beylic that was from these beylics developed rapidly after 1299 and possessed Anatolia. They established a powerful state on these lands and continued the activities for centuries from the aspect of handicrafts.

HACIBEKTAŞ

Hacıbektaş, that was also known formerly as "Suluca Karahöyük", is forty-five kilometers to the north of Nevşehir. It is understood from the excavations made here that previously it was under the occupation of the Hittites, Phrygians, Romans and Byzantines.

In the thirteenth century Hacı Bektaş-ı Veli, who came from Horasan, made a dervish lodge here. Later it became a dervish center.

Here a large quantity of food was prepared and would be distributed to the hungry and the poor. The Islamic religion was spreading as well while Hacı Bektaş-ı Veli was doing this. A large group of people believed in him and became Moslems. He was buried here when he died and the name of the area became Hacıbektaş.

In the fourteenth century a small house was constructed for a dervish's period of retirement and fasting, that lasted forty days, and it was enlarged later. The first restoration activities were undertaken in the nineteenth century. It was restored by the General Directorate of Antiquities and Museums between 1954 to 1966 and opened to the public.

A Hacı Bektaş-ı Veli Festival is held annually between 16 to 18 August.

OLD HANDMADE ARTIFACTS IN ANATOLIA

Old handmade artifacts in various regions in Anatolia were used up until a recent period in history. They have now lost their currency and have been replaced with modern items and materials. Many of these have been taken and placed in museums.

Even so, in some regions these extraordinary and handmade items have continued to be used up until today and are still maintaining their prevalence.

A large mortar for crushing bulgur.

A two-wheeled transport vehicle (Oxcart).

Churn.

Dough spatula.

Coffee roasters.

Sheet iron stand.

Copper water pitcher.

Dipper.

Coffee box.

Dough tray (Bread tray).

Churn.

Large mortar.

Small, long-handled
pot for making
Turkish coffee.

Water container
(made of wood).

Pieces for a carpet weaving loom.

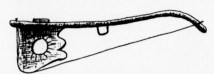

Wool fluffing instrument.

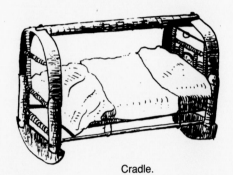

Cradle.

Kilim motifs at Cappadocia.

Torch stand.

Thread twisting instrument.

Mittens.

Wool spindle to spin wool.

Small bag.

Kilim motifs at Cappadocia.

Container for placing
an oil lamp.